# Final Determination on the Appropriateness of the Model Year 2022-2025 Light-Duty Vehicle Greenhouse Gas Emissions Standards under the Midterm Evaluation

U.S. Environmental Protection Agency

EPA-420-R-17-001
January 2017

**Table of Contents**

## Executive Summary

The 2012 rulemaking establishing the National Program for federal greenhouse gas (GHG) emissions and corporate average fuel economy (CAFE) standards for model years (MY)2017-2025 light-duty vehicles included a regulatory requirement for the Environmental Protection Agency (EPA) to conduct a Midterm Evaluation (MTE) of the GHG standards established for model years (MY)2022-2025.[1] In this final order, the Administrator is making a final adjudicatory determination (hereafter "determination") that, based on her evaluation of extensive technical information available to her and significant input from the industry and other stakeholders, and in light of the factors listed in the 2012 final rule establishing the MY2017-2025 standards, the MY2022-2025 standards remain appropriate under section 202 (a) (1) of the Clean Air Act. This action leaves those standards entirely as they now exist, unaltered. The regulatory status quo is unchanged. This final order constitutes a final agency action. See 76 FR 48763 (Aug. 9, 2011).

This Final Determination follows the November 2016 Proposed Determination issued by the EPA Administrator and the July 2016 release of a Draft Technical Assessment Report (TAR), issued jointly by the EPA, the National Highway Traffic Safety Administration (NHTSA), and the California Air Resources Board (CARB). Opportunities for public comment were provided for both the Draft TAR and the Proposed Determination. In the Draft TAR, the agencies examined a wide range of issues relevant to GHG emissions standards for MY2022-2025, and shared with the public their initial technical analyses of those issues. The Draft TAR was required by EPA's regulations as the first step in the Midterm Evaluation process. In developing the Proposed Determination, the Administrator considered public comments on the Draft TAR and EPA updated its analyses where appropriate in response to comments and to reflect the latest available data. The Administrator has likewise considered public input on the Proposed Determination in developing this Final Determination.

As the final step in the MTE, the Administrator must determine whether the MY2022-2025 GHG standards, established in 2012, are still appropriate under section 202(a)(1) of the Clean Air Act (Act), in light of the record before the Administrator, given the latest available data and information. EPA's regulations establish April 1, 2018, as the latest date for such a determination, but otherwise do not constrain the Administrator's discretion to select an earlier determination date. The Administrator is choosing to make the Final Determination now, recognizing that long-term regulatory certainty and stability are important for the automotive industry and will contribute to the continued success of the program, which in turn will reduce emissions, improve fuel economy, deliver significant fuel savings to consumers, and benefit public health and welfare.

EPA received more than 100,000 public comments on the Proposed Determination, with comments from about 60 organizations and the rest from individuals. These public comments have informed the Administrator's Final Determination, and EPA has responded to those comments in the accompanying Response to Comments (RTC) document. This record[2]

---

[1] 40 CFR 86.1818-12(h).

[2] This record, the basis for the Administrator's determination, is contained in EPA Docket ID No. EPA-HQ-OAR-2015-0827.

represents the most current information available, as informed by public comment, and provides the basis for the Administrator's Final Determination, as called for in the 2012 rule.

The EPA regulations state that in making the required determination, the Administrator shall consider the information available on the factors relevant to setting greenhouse gas emission standards under section 202(a) of the Clean Air Act for model years 2022 through 2025, including but not limited to:

- The availability and effectiveness of technology, and the appropriate lead time for introduction of technology;

- The cost on the producers or purchasers of new motor vehicles or new motor vehicle engines;

- The feasibility and practicability of the standards;

- The impact of the standards on reduction of emissions, oil conservation, energy security, and fuel savings by consumers;

- The impact of the standards on the automobile industry;

- The impacts of the standards on automobile safety;

- The impact of the greenhouse gas emission standards on the Corporate Average Fuel Economy standards and a national harmonized program; and

- The impact of the standards on other relevant factors.[3]

This Final Determination is the Administrator's final decision on whether or not the MY2022-2025 standards are appropriate under section 202(a)(1) of the Clean Air Act, in light of the record now before the Administrator. EPA's regulations specify that the determination shall be "based upon a record that includes the following:

- A Draft Technical Assessment Report addressing issues relevant to the standard for the 2022 through 2025 model years;

- Public comment on the Draft Technical Assessment Report;

- Public comment on whether the standards established for the 2022 through 2025 model years are appropriate under section 202(a) of the Clean Air Act; and

- Such other materials the Administrator deems appropriate."[4]

The EPA has now concluded all the required steps in the MTE process and the record upon which the Administrator is making this Final Determination reflects all the elements specified in the regulations. As discussed above, EPA issued (jointly with NHTSA and CARB) the July 2016 Draft Technical Assessment Report (TAR) and sought public comment on it. EPA updated

---

[3] 40 CFR 86.1818-12(h)(1).
[4] 40 CFR 86.1818-12(h)(2).

its Draft TAR assessment in response to public comments as part of the November 2016 Proposed Determination. EPA also sought public comment on the Proposed Determination that the GHG standards for MY2022-2025 remain appropriate under section 202 (a)(1) of the Act. If those comments had included information that led the Administrator to the determination that the standards are inappropriate, EPA would then have had to initiate a rulemaking seeking to amend those standards, as specified in the MTE regulation.[5] However, no factual evidence came to light in the public comments or otherwise that leads the Administrator to a different conclusion than the one set forth in the Proposed Determination. The Administrator is thus making this Final Determination that the standards remain appropriate, and that no further action under the Midterm Evaluation is necessary. Thus the standards remain unchanged and the regulatory status quo is unaltered. See also 76 FR 48763 (Aug. 9, 2011) ("[t]he MY2022-2025 GHG standards will remain in effect unless and until EPA changes them by rulemaking").

EPA's updated analyses presented in the Proposed Determination built upon and were directly responsive to public comments on the Draft TAR. The Administrator has fully considered public comments submitted in response to the Proposed Determination, and EPA has responded to comments in the accompanying Response to Comments (RTC) document. The Administrator believes that there has been no information presented in the public comments on the Proposed Determination that materially changes the Agency's analysis documented in the Proposed Determination. Therefore, the Administrator considers the analyses presented in the Proposed Determination[6] as the final EPA analyses upon which her Final Determination is based.

The Administrator notes that, in response to EPA's solicitation of comment on the topic, several commenters spoke to the need for additional incentives or flexibilities in the out years of the program including incentives that could continue to help promote the market for very advanced technologies, such as electric vehicles. She notes that her determination, based on the record before her, is that the MY2022-2025 standards currently in effect are feasible (evaluated against the criteria established in the 2012 rule) and appropriate under section 202, and do not need to be revised. This conclusion, however, neither precludes nor prejudices the possibility of a future rulemaking to provide additional incentives for very clean technologies or flexibilities that could assist manufacturers with longer term planning without compromising the effectiveness of the current program. The EPA is always open to further dialogue with the manufacturers, NHTSA, CARB and other stakeholders to explore and consider the suggestions made to date and any other ideas that could enhance firms' incentives to move forward with and to help promote the market for very advanced technologies, such as electric vehicles (EVs), plug-in hybrid electric vehicles (PHEVs), and fuel cell vehicles (FCEVs).

The basis for the Administrator's assessment supporting her decision that the MY2022-2025 standards are appropriate is summarized below.

*The Standards Are Feasible at Reasonable Cost, Without Need for Extensive Electrification.* As part of our technical assessment of the technologies available to meet the MY2022-2025 GHG standards, we present a range of feasible, cost-effective compliance pathways to meet the

---

[5] 40 CFR 86.1818-12(h) (final sentence).

[6] Proposed Determination on the Appropriateness of the Model Year 2022-2025 Light-Duty Vehicle Greenhouse Gas Emissions Standards under the Midterm Evaluation, EPA-420-R-16-020, and accompanying Technical Support Document, EPA-420-R-16-021, November 2016.

MY2022-2025 standards. This analysis demonstrates that compliance can be achieved through a number of different technology pathways reflecting predominantly the application of technologies already in commercial production. The EPA also considered further developments in technologies where there is reliable evidence that those technologies could be feasibly deployed by 2025. The standards are in fact devised so as not to force manufacturers into a single compliance path, and the analysis showing multiple compliance pathways indicates that the standards provide each manufacturer with the flexibility to apply technologies in the way it views best to meet the needs of its customers. Moreover, given the rapid pace of automotive industry innovation, we believe there are, and will continue to be, emerging technologies that will be available in the MY2022-2025 time frame that could perform appreciably better at potentially lower cost than the technologies modeled in EPA's assessment. We have already seen this type of innovative development since the MY2017-2025 GHG standards were originally promulgated in 2012, including expanded use of continuously variable transmissions and introduction of higher expansion ratio, naturally aspirated gasoline engines (Atkinson). Updated information also shows that some of the technologies we did anticipate in 2012 are costing less, and are more effective, than we anticipated at that time.

EPA further projects that the MY2022-2025 standards can be met largely through advances in gasoline vehicle technologies, such as improvements in engines, transmissions, light-weighting, aerodynamics, and accessories, and, as noted, that there are multiple available compliance pathways based on the predominant use of these technologies. This analysis is consistent with both agencies' findings in the 2012 final rulemaking (FRM). Table ES-1 shows fleet-wide penetration rates for a subset of the technologies EPA projects could be used to comply with the MY2025 standards. The analyses further indicate that very low levels of strong hybrids and electric vehicles (both plug-in hybrid electric vehicles (PHEV) and electric vehicles (EV)) will be needed to meet the standards. EPA analyzed a central case low-cost pathway as well as multiple sensitivity cases, all of which show that compliance can be achieved through a number of different technology pathways without extensive use of strong hybrid or electric vehicles. These sensitivity cases include various fuel price scenarios, cost markups, and technology penetrations (e.g., lower Atkinson penetration, lower mass reduction, alternative transmissions). See Table ES-1, presenting the sensitivity cases as a range of technology penetrations and per-vehicle costs. These costs are lower than those projected in the 2012 rule; at that time, the EPA projected that average per-vehicle costs, although reasonable, would be about $1,100.[7]

**Table ES-1 Selected Technology Penetrations (Absolute) and Per-Vehicle Average Costs (2015$) to Meet MY2025 GHG Standards (Incremental to the Costs to Meet the MY2021 Standards)[1]**

| | Final Determination | |
| --- | --- | --- |
| | Primary Analysis | Range of Sensitivities Analyzed |
| Turbocharged and downsized gasoline engines (%) | 34% | 31 - 41% |
| Higher expansion ratio, naturally aspirated gasoline engines (%) | 27% | 5 - 41% |
| 8 speed and other advanced transmissions[2] (%) | 93% | 92 - 94% |
| Mass reduction (%) | 9% | 2 - 10% |

---

[7] 77 FR 62853, October 15, 2012; Draft Technical Assessment Report, Table 12.44.

| | | |
|---|---|---|
| Off-cycle technology[3] | 26% | 13 - 51% |
| Stop-start (%) | 15% | 12 - 39% |
| Mild Hybrid (%) | 18% | 16 - 27% |
| Strong Hybrid (%) | 2% | 2 - 3% |
| Plug-in hybrid electric vehicle[4] (%) | 2% | 2% |
| Electric vehicle[4] (%) | 3% | 2 - 4% |
| **Per vehicle cost (2015$)** | **$875** | **$800 - $1,115** |

Notes:

[1] Percentages shown are absolute rather than incremental. Values based on AEO 2016 reference case.

[2] Including continuously variable transmissions (CVT).

[3] In addition to modeling the off-cycle credits of stop-start and active aerodynamics, EPA also assessed additional off-cycle technologies as unique technologies that can be applied to a vehicle and that reduce $CO_2$ emissions by either 1.5 g/mi or 3 g/mi. See Proposed Determination Appendix C.1.1.1.3,

[4] Electric vehicle penetrations include the California Zero Emission Vehicle (ZEV) program.

*The Standards Will Achieve Significant $CO_2$ and Oil Reductions.* Based on various assumptions, including the U.S. Department of Energy's Annual Energy Outlook (AEO) 2016 reference case projections of the car/truck mix out to 2025, the footprint-based GHG standards curves for MY2022-2025 are projected to achieve an industry-wide fleet average carbon dioxide ($CO_2$) target of 173 grams/mile (g/mi) in MY2025 (Table ES-2). The projected fleet average $CO_2$ target represents a 2-cycle GHG emissions compliance level equivalent to 51.4 mpg-e (if all reductions were achieved exclusively through fuel economy improvements).[8] EPA projects that this GHG compliance level of 51.4 mpg-e could be met by automakers with average real world/label fuel economy of about 36 mpg. Given that the MY2016 real world fleet average fuel economy is about 26 mpg, this means that the fleet must improve real world fuel economy by about 10 mpg over the 9-year period from 2016 to 2025, or about one mpg per year.[9]

As a sensitivity, Table ES-2 also includes target projections based on two AEO 2016 scenarios in addition to the AEO 2016 reference case: a low fuel price case and a high fuel price case. Under the footprint-based standards, the program is designed to ensure significant GHG reductions across the fleet, and each automaker's standard automatically adjusts based on the mix (size and volume) of vehicles it produces each model year. Thus, as shown in Table ES-2, different fuel price cases translate into different projections for the car/truck fleet mix (e.g., with a higher truck share shown in the low fuel price case, and a lower truck share shown in the high fuel price case), which in turn leads to varying projections for the $CO_2$ targets and MPG-e levels projected for MY2025. These estimated $CO_2$ target levels reflect changes in the latest projections about the MY2025 fleet mix compared to the projections in 2012 when the standards were first established.

In our analysis for this Final Determination, we are applying the same footprint-based curves to the updated fleet projections for MY2025. It is important to keep in mind that the updated

[8] The projected MY2025 target of 173 g/mi represents an approximate 50 percent decrease in GHG emissions relative to the fuel economy standards that were in place in 2010. It is clear from current GHG manufacturer performance data that many automakers are earning air conditioner refrigerant GHG credits that reduce GHG emissions, but do not improve fuel economy. Accordingly, the projected MY2025 target of 173 g/mi represents slightly less than a doubling of fuel economy relative to the standards that were in place in 2010.

[9] U.S. EPA, Light-Duty Automotive Technology, Carbon Dioxide Emissions, and Fuel Economy Trends: 1975 Through 2016," November 2016, www.epa.gov/fuel-economy/trends-report.

MY2025 fleet wide projections reflected in this Final Determination are still projections-- based on the latest available information, which will likely continue to change with future projections -- and that the actual GHG emissions/fuel economy level achieved in MY2025 will not be determined until the manufacturers have completed their MY2025 production. Put another way, each manufacturer will not know what its individual standard is until MY2025, since that individual standard is determined by the type and number of vehicles the manufacturer chooses to produce.

**Table ES-2  Projections for MY2025:  Car/Truck Mix, $CO_2$ Target Levels, and MPG-equivalent[1]**

|  | 2012 Final Rule | Final Determination | | |
|---|---|---|---|---|
|  | AEO 2011 Reference | **AEO 2016 Reference** | AEO 2016 Low | AEO 2016 High |
| Fuel Price in 2025 ($/gallon)[2] | $3.87 | **$2.97** | $1.97 | $4.94 |
| Car/truck mix | 67/33% | **53/47%** | 44/56% | 63/37% |
| $CO_2$ (g/mi) | 163 | **173** | 178 | 167 |
| MPG-e[3] | 54.5 | **51.4** | 49.9 | 53.3 |

Notes:

[1] The $CO_2$ and MPG-e values shown here are 2-cycle compliance values.  Projected real-world values are detailed in the Proposed Determination TSD Chapter 3; for example, AEO reference fuel price case, real-world $CO_2$ emissions performance would be 233 g/mi and real-world fuel economy would be about 36 mpg.

[2] AEO 2011 fuel price is 2010$ (equivalent to $4.21 in 2015$); AEO 2016 fuel prices are 2015$.

[3] Mile per gallon equivalent (MPG-e) is the corresponding fleet average fuel economy value if the entire fleet were to meet the $CO_2$ standard compliance level through tailpipe $CO_2$ improvements that also improve fuel economy. This is provided for illustrative purposes only, as we do not expect the GHG standards to be met only with fuel efficiency technology.

EPA estimates that over the vehicle lifetimes the MY2022-2025 standards will reduce GHG emissions by 540 million metric tons and reduce oil consumption by 1.2 billion barrels, as shown in Table ES-3.

**Table ES-3  Cumulative GHG and Oil Reductions for Meeting the MY2022-2025 Standards (Vehicle Lifetime Reductions)**

|  | Final Determination[1] |
|---|---|
| GHG reduction (million metric tons, MMT $CO_2e$) | 540 |
| Oil reduction (billion barrels) | 1.2 |

Note:

[1] Values based on AEO 2016 reference case.

*The Standards Will Provide Significant Benefits to Consumers and to the Public.*  The net benefits of the MY2022-2025 standards are nearly $100 billion (at 3 percent discount rate). Table ES-4 presents the societal monetized benefits associated with meeting the MY2022-2025 standards.  The EPA also evaluated the benefit-costs of additional scenarios (AEO 2016 high and low fuel price scenarios).  See Proposed Determination Section IV.A.  In all cases, the net benefits far exceed the costs of the program.  It is also notable that in all cases, the benefits (excluding fuel savings) and the fuel savings, each independently, exceed the costs.  That is, the benefits exceed the costs without considering any fuel savings, and likewise fuel savings exceed the costs even without considering any other benefits.

Table ES-4  GHG Analysis of Lifetime Costs & Benefits to Meet the MY2022-2025 GHG Standards (for Vehicles Produced in MY2021-2025)[1] (Billions of $)

| | Final Determination[2] | |
|---|---|---|
| | 3 Percent Discount Rate | 7 Percent Discount Rate |
| Vehicle Program | -$33 | -$24 |
| Maintenance | -$3 | -$2 |
| Fuel | $92 | $52 |
| Benefits[1] | $42 | $32 |
| Net Benefits | $98 | $59 |

Notes:
[1] All values are discounted back to 2016. See the Proposed Determination Appendix C for details on discounting social cost of GHG and non-GHG benefits, and for a discussion that the costs and benefits reflect some early compliance with the MY2025 standard in MY2021.
[2] Values based on AEO 2016 reference case and 2015$.

When considering the payback of an average MY2025 vehicle compared to a vehicle meeting the MY2021 standards, we believe one of the most meaningful analyses is to look at the payback for consumers who finance their vehicle, as the vast majority of consumers (nearly 86 percent) purchase new vehicles through financing. The average loan period is over 67 months. Consumers who finance their vehicle with a 5-year loan would see payback within the first year. Consumers who pay cash for their vehicle would see payback in the fifth year of ownership. Consumers would realize net savings of $1,650 over the lifetime of their new vehicle (i.e., net of increased lifetime costs and lifetime fuel savings). Even with the lowest fuel prices projected by AEO 2016 (see Proposed Determination Appendix C), approximately $2 per gallon in 2025, the lifetime fuel savings significantly outweigh the increased lifetime costs.

Table ES-5  Payback Period and Net Lifetime Consumer Savings for an Average MY2025 Vehicle Compared to the MY2021 GHG Standards

| | Final Determination[1] |
|---|---|
| Payback period – 5-year loan purchase[2] (years) | <1 |
| Payback period – Cash purchase (years) | 5 |
| Net Lifetime Consumer Savings ($, discounted at 3%) | $1,650 |

Notes:
[1] Values based on AEO 2016 reference case and 2015$
[2] Using an interest rate of 4.25 percent.

*The Auto Industry is Thriving and Meeting the Standards More Quickly than Required.* While the Final Determination focuses on the MY2022-2025 standards, we note that the auto industry, on average, has out-performed the first four years of the light-duty GHG standards (MY2012-2015). This has occurred concurrently with a period during which the industry successfully rebounded after a period of economic distress. The recently released GHG Manufacturer

Performance Report for the 2015 Model Year shows that the National Program is working even at low fuel prices and automakers are over-complying with the standards, notwithstanding that the MY2015 standard was the most stringent to date, and that the increase in stringency from the previous model year was also the most pronounced to date.[10] Further, concurrently with out-performing the GHG standards, sales have increased for seven straight years, for the first time in 100 years, to an all-time record high in 2016, reflecting positive consumer response to vehicles meeting the standards.

The Administrator's Final Determination is that the MY2022-2025 standards remain appropriate. In light of the pace of progress in reducing GHG emissions since the MY2022-2025 standards were adopted, the success of automakers in achieving the standards to date while vehicle sales are strong, the projected costs of the standards, the impact of the standards on reducing emissions and fuel costs for consumers, and the other factors identified in 40 CFR 86.1818-12(h), the Administrator concludes that the record does not support a conclusion that the MY2022-2025 standards should be revised to make them less stringent. The Administrator did consider whether it would be appropriate to propose to amend the standards to increase their stringency. In her view, the current record, including the current state of technology and the pace of technology development and implementation, could support a proposal, and potentially an ultimate decision, to adopt more stringent standards for MY2022-2025. However, she also recognizes that regulatory certainty and consequent stability is important, and that it is important not to disrupt the industry's long-term planning. Long lead time is needed to accommodate significant redesigns. The Administrator also believes a decision to maintain the current standards provides support to a timely NHTSA rulemaking to adopt MY2022-2025 standards, as well as to the California Air Resources Board to consider in its review of the California GHG vehicle standards for MY2022-2025 as part of its Advanced Clean Cars program,[11] and thus to a harmonized national program. The Administrator consequently has concluded that it is appropriate to provide the full measure of lead time for the MY2022-2025 standards, rather than adopting (or, more precisely, proposing to adopt) new, more stringent standards with a shorter lead time.

---

[10] "Greenhouse Gas Emission Standards for Light-duty Vehicles, Manufacturer Performance Report for the 2015 Model Year, November 2016, EPA-420-R-16-014.https://www.epa.gov/regulations-emissions-vehicles-and-engines/ghg-emission-standards-light-duty-vehicles-manufacturer.

[11] California adopted its own GHG standards for MY2017-2025 in 2012 prior to EPA and NHTSA finalizing the National Program. Through direction from its Board in 2012, CARB both adopted a "deemed to comply" provision allowing compliance with EPA's GHG standards in lieu of CARB's standards, and committed to participate in the Midterm Evaluation (https://www.arb.ca.gov/msprog/consumer_info/advanced_clean_cars/consumer_acc_mtr.htm).

# I.    Introduction

## A.    Background on the Midterm Evaluation

The Environmental Protection Agency (EPA) and the National Highway Traffic Safety Administration (NHTSA) have conducted two joint rulemakings to establish a coordinated National Program for federal greenhouse gas (GHG) emissions and corporate average fuel economy (CAFE) standards for light-duty vehicles.  Light-duty vehicles, which include passenger cars, sport utility vehicles, crossover utility vehicles, minivans, and pickup trucks, make up about 60 percent of all U.S. transportation-related GHG emissions and fuel consumption.[12]  The agencies finalized the first set of National Program standards covering model years (MYs) 2012-2016 in May 2010[13] and the second set of standards, covering MY2017-2025, in October 2012.[14]  The National Program is one of the most significant federal actions ever taken to reduce domestic GHG emissions and improve automotive fuel economy, establishing standards that increase in stringency year-over-year from MY2012 through MY2025 and projected to reach a level that nearly doubles fuel economy and halves GHG emissions compared to MY2010.

Through the coordination of the National Program with the California Air Resources Board's GHG standards, automakers can build one single fleet of vehicles across the U.S. that satisfies all GHG/CAFE requirements, and consumers can continue to have a full range of vehicle choices that meet their needs.[15]  In addition, the Canadian government has adopted standards aligned with the U.S. EPA GHG standards through MY2025, further facilitating manufacturers' ability to produce vehicles satisfying harmonized standards.[16]  Most stakeholders strongly supported the National Program, including the auto industry, automotive suppliers, state and local governments, labor unions, NGOs, consumer groups, veterans groups, and others.  In the agencies' 2012 final rules, the National Program was estimated to reduce carbon dioxide ($CO_2$) emissions by 6 billion metric tons and reduce oil consumption by 12 billion barrels over the lifetime of MY2012-2025 vehicles.  The standards are projected to provide significant savings for consumers due to reduced fuel use and consequent reduced fuel expenditures.

The 2012 final rule established standards through MY2025 to provide substantial lead time and regulatory certainty to the industry.  Recognizing the rule's long time frame, EPA's rule establishing GHG standards for MY2017-2025 light-duty vehicles included a requirement for the agency to conduct a Midterm Evaluation (MTE) of the MYs 2022-2025 GHG standards.  Through the MTE, EPA must determine whether the GHG standards for MY2022-2025,

---

[12] Inventory of U.S. Greenhouse Gas Emissions and Sinks: 1990-2014, EPA Publication number EPA 430-R-16-002, April 15, 2016.  Overall transportation sources account for 26 percent of total U.S. GHG emissions.

[13] 75 FR 25324, May 7, 2010.

[14] 77 FR 62624, October 15, 2012.

[15] Subsequent to the adoption of California-specific GHG standards for MYs 2017-2025 and the adoption of the Federal standards for MY2017 and beyond, CARB adopted a "deemed to comply" provision in furtherance of a National Program whereby compliance with the federal GHG standards would be deemed to be compliance with California's GHG program.

[16] EPA has coordinated with Environment and Climate Change Canada (ECCC) and Transport Canada throughout the Midterm Evaluation, including collaborating on a number of technology research projects.  See Draft Technical Assessment Report Chapter 2.2.3, p. 2-8.

established in 2012, are still appropriate, within the meaning of section 202(a)(1) of the Clean Air Act, in light of the record before the Administrator, given the latest available data and information. See 40 CFR 86.1818-12(h). The MTE regulations provide that if the Administrator were to make a determination that the standards are not appropriate, based upon consideration of the decision factors in the regulation and the factual record available to the Administrator at the time of the determination, then the EPA would initiate a rulemaking to amend the standards to make them either more or less stringent. See 40 CFR 86.1818-12(h) (final sentence). This regulatory provision to conduct a rulemaking is limited only to the situation where the Administrator makes a determination that the standards are not appropriate and should be changed, to be either more or less stringent, and not to the situation where the Administrator, as in the case of this Final Determination, determines that the standards are appropriate and should not be changed. See 77 FR 62784 (Oct. 15, 2012) (stating that if EPA concludes the standards are appropriate it will "announce that final decision and the basis for EPA's decision" and if the EPA decides the standards are not appropriate, it will "initiate a rulemaking to adopt standards that are appropriate under section 202(a)").

In the 2012 rulemaking, the EPA stated its intention that the MTE would entail "a holistic assessment of all of the factors considered in standards setting," and "the expected impact of those factors on manufacturers' ability to comply, without placing decisive weight on any particular factor or projection." See 77 FR 62784 (Oct. 15, 2012). Indeed, the analyses supporting this MTE have been as robust and comprehensive as that in the original setting of the MY2017-2025 standards, *Id.,* although the nature of the decision-making the EPA has undertaken based on those analyses is very different, as established by design of the MTE regulations. In the 2012 rule, the EPA was faced with establishing the MY2017-2025 standards, while in this Final Determination the EPA has evaluated those standards in light of developments to date in order to determine if the existing standards are appropriate. *Id.* In gathering data and information throughout the MTE process, the EPA has drawn from a wide range of sources, including vehicle certification data, research projects and vehicle testing programs initiated by the agencies, input from stakeholders, and information from technical conferences, published literature, studies published by various organizations, and the many public comments.

In July 2016, EPA, NHTSA, and CARB jointly issued for public comment a Draft Technical Assessment Report (TAR) examining a wide range of issues relevant to the MY2022-2025 standards.[17] For the EPA, the Draft TAR was the first formal step in the MTE process as required under EPA's regulations.[18] The Draft TAR was a technical report, not a decision document. It was an opportunity for all three agencies to share with the public their technical analyses relating to the appropriateness of the MY2022-2025 standards.

The EPA received over 200,000 public comments on the Draft TAR, including about 90 comments from organizations and the rest from individuals. The organization commenters included auto manufacturers and suppliers, environmental and other non-governmental organizations (NGOs), consumer groups, state and local governments and their associations, labor unions, fuels and energy providers, auto dealers, academics, national security experts,

---

[17] 81 FR 49217, July 27, 2016.
[18] See 40 CFR 86.1818-12(h)(2)(i).

veteran's groups, and others. These comments presented a range of views on whether the standards should be retained, or made more or less stringent, and, in some cases, provided additional factual information that EPA considered in updating its analyses in support of the Administrator's Proposed Determination. The EPA also considered the few additional comments received after the close of the comment period on the Draft TAR.[19]

On November 30, 2016, EPA Administrator issued a proposed adjudicatory determination[20] proposing to find that the MY2022-2025 standards remain appropriate under the Clean Air Act. Because the Administrator was proposing that there be no change to the MY2022-2025 standards currently in the regulations, in other words that there be no change in the standards' stringency, the Proposed Determination did not include a Notice of Proposed Rulemaking. See section 86.1818-12(h). In this Final Determination, the Administrator has once again considered public comments -- those received on the Proposed Determination. The EPA received more than 100,000 comments on the Proposed Determination, with about 60 comments from organizations and the rest from individuals. The EPA responds to the public comments in the accompanying Response to Comments (RTC) document.

The EPA regulations state that in making the required determination, the Administrator shall consider the information available on the factors relevant to setting greenhouse gas emission standards under section 202(a) of the Clean Air Act for model years 2022 through 2025, including but not limited to:

- The availability and effectiveness of technology, and the appropriate lead time for introduction of technology;
- The cost on the producers or purchasers of new motor vehicles or new motor vehicle engines;
- The feasibility and practicability of the standards;
- The impact of the standards on reduction of emissions, oil conservation, energy security, and fuel savings by consumers;
- The impact of the standards on the automobile industry;

---

[19] After the close of the comment period on the Draft TAR, EPA received and docketed additional comments from Volkswagen, the Electric Drive Transportation Association, and the Alliance of Automobile Manufacturers (a non-technical comment), all of which the EPA considered in the Proposed Determination.

[20] As noted in the Proposed Determination, and discussed more fully in the Response to Comments, the determination is not a rulemaking. None of EPA's rules, the Administrative Procedures Act, or the Clean Air Act require that the determination be made by rulemaking. EPA is properly exercising its discretion to proceed by adjudication. The final determination evaluates the technical record and concludes that the current standards are appropriate. As with past mid-course evaluations of Title II rules, where the EPA evaluates standards and decides not to change them, it need not undertake, and is not undertaking, a rulemaking. For example, in the final rule for heavy-duty engine standards (66 FR 5063, January 18, 2001), EPA announced regular biennial reviews of the status of the key emission control technology. EPA subsequently issued those reviews in 2002 and 2004, without going through rulemaking. See EPA Report 420-R-02-016; EPA Report 420-R-04-004. Or for instance, in the final rule for the Nonroad Tier 3 standards (63 FR 56983, Oct 23, 1998), EPA committed to reviewing the feasibility of the standards by 2001 and to adjust them by rulemaking if necessary. In 2001, without engaging in rulemaking, the EPA published a report, see EPA Report 420-R-01-052, accepted comments, and concluded publicly that the standards remained technologically feasible. (Memorandum: "Comments On Nonroad Diesel Emissions Standards: Staff Technical Paper," from Chet France to Margo Oge, June 4, 2002).

- The impacts of the standards on automobile safety;
- The impact of the greenhouse gas emission standards on the Corporate Average Fuel Economy standards and a national harmonized program; and
- The impact of the standards on other relevant factors.[21]

The preamble to the 2012 final rule further listed ten relevant factors that the agencies will consider at a minimum during the MTE. The EPA in fact addressed all of these issues in the Draft TAR, and considered them further in the Proposed Determination and in this Final Determination.[22]

- Development of powertrain improvements to gasoline and diesel powered vehicles;
- Impacts on employment, including the auto sector;
- Availability and implementation of methods to reduce weight, including any impacts on safety;
- Actual and projected availability of public and private charging infrastructure for electric vehicles, and fueling infrastructure for alternative fueled vehicles;
- Costs, availability, and consumer acceptance of technologies to ensure compliance with the standards, such as vehicle batteries and power electronics, mass reduction, and anticipated trends in these costs;
- Payback periods for any incremental vehicle costs associated with meeting the standards;
- Costs for gasoline, diesel fuel, and alternative fuels;
- Total light-duty vehicle sales and projected fleet mix;
- Market penetration across the fleet of fuel efficient technologies;
- Any other factors that may be deemed relevant to the review.[23]

In the 2012 final rule, the agencies projected that the MY2025 standards would be met largely through advances in conventional vehicle technologies, including advances in gasoline engines (such as downsized/turbocharged engines) and transmissions, vehicle weight reduction, improvements in aerodynamics, more efficient accessories, and lower rolling resistance tires. The agencies also projected that vehicle air conditioning systems would continue to improve by becoming more efficient and by increasing the use of alternative refrigerants and lower leakage systems. The EPA estimated that some increased electrification of the fleet would occur through the expanded use of stop/start and mild hybrid technologies, but projected that the MY2025 standards could be met with only about five percent of the fleet being strong hybrid electric vehicles (HEVs) and only about two percent of the fleet to be electric vehicles (EV) or plug-in hybrid electric vehicles (PHEVs).[24] All of these technologies were available at the time of the

---

[21] 40 CFR 86.1818-12(h).

[22] 76 FR 48673 (Aug. 9, 2011) and 77 FR 62784, October 15, 2012.

[23] Among the other factors deemed relevant and addressed in the Draft TAR and Proposed Determination, EPA's analysis examined the potential impact of the California Zero Emission Vehicle (ZEV) program, which California has revised since the 2012 final rule. EPA also examined the availability and use of credits, including credits for emission reductions from air conditioning improvements and from off-cycle technologies.

[24] For comparison to vehicles for sale today, an example of a mild HEV is GM's eAssist (Buick Lacrosse), a strong HEV is the Toyota Prius, an EV is the Nissan Leaf, and a PHEV is the Chevrolet Volt.

2012 final rule, some on a limited number of vehicles while others were more widespread, and the agencies projected that manufacturers would be able to meet the standards through significant efficiency improvements in the technologies, as well as through increased usage of these and other technologies across the fleet.

Since the 2012 final rule, vehicle sales have been strong, hitting an all-time high of 17.5 million vehicles in 2015, gas prices have dropped significantly, and truck share of the fleet has increased. At the same time, auto manufacturers have over-complied with the GHG program for each of the first four years of the program (MY2012-2015), and the industry as a whole has built a substantial bank of credits from the initial years of the program.[25] Technologies that reduce GHG emissions are entering the market at rapid rates, including more efficient engines and transmissions, aerodynamics, light-weighting, improved accessories, low rolling resistance tires, improved air conditioning systems, and others. Manufacturers are also using certain technologies that the agencies did not consider in their evaluation in the 2012 rule, including non-hybrid Atkinson cycle gasoline engines and 48-volt mild hybrid systems. Other technologies are being utilized at greater rates than the agencies projected, such as continuously variable transmissions (CVTs). These additional technologies have resulted in projected compliance pathways which differ slightly from those in the 2012 final rule with respect to some of the specific technologies expected to be applied to meet the future standards. However, the conclusions of the 2012 Final Rule, the July 2016 Draft TAR, the November 2016 Proposed Determination, and this Final Determination are very similar: that advanced gasoline vehicles will be the predominant technologies that manufacturers can use to meet the MY2025 standards. This assessment is similar to the conclusion of a 2015 study by the National Academy of Sciences which also found that the 2025 standards could be achieved primarily with advanced gasoline vehicle technologies.[26] As discussed below, the standards are also projected to be achievable through multiple feasible technology pathways at reasonable cost -- less than projected in the 2012 rulemaking -- and with significant direct benefit to consumers in the form of net savings due to purchasing less fuel.

The Administrator notes that, in response to EPA's solicitation of comment on the topic, several commenters spoke to the need for additional incentives or flexibilities in the out years of the program including incentives that could continue to help promote the market for very advanced technologies, such as electric vehicles. She notes that her determination, based on the record before her, is that the MY2022-2025 standards currently in effect are feasible (evaluated against the criteria established in the 2012 rule) and appropriate under section 202, and do not need to be revised. This conclusion, however, neither precludes nor prejudices the possibility of a future rulemaking to provide additional incentives for very clean technologies or flexibilities that could assist manufacturers with longer term planning without compromising the effectiveness of the current program. The EPA is always open to further dialog with the manufacturers, NHTSA, CARB and other stakeholders to explore and consider the suggestions made to date and any other ideas that could enhance firms' incentives to move forward with and

---

[25] "Greenhouse Gas Emission Standards for Light-duty Vehicles, Manufacturer Performance Report for the 2015 Model Year, November 2016, EPA-420-R-16-014.

[26] "Cost, Effectiveness and Deployment of Fuel Economy Technologies for Light-Duty Vehicles," National Research Council of the National Academies, June 2015, Finding 2.1 (p. 2-83).

to help promote the market for very advanced technologies, such as electric vehicles (EVs), plug-in hybrid electric vehicles (PHEVs), and fuel cell vehicles (FCEVs).

## B. Background on the Light-duty Vehicle GHG Standards

The GHG emissions standards are attribute-based standards, based on vehicle footprint.[27] In other words, the standards are based on a vehicle's size: larger vehicles have numerically higher GHG emissions targets and smaller vehicles have numerically lower GHG emissions targets. Manufacturers are not compelled to build vehicles of any particular size or type, and each manufacturer has a unique fleetwide standard for each of its car and truck fleets that reflects the light-duty vehicles it chooses to produce in a given model year. Each automaker's standard automatically adjusts each year based on the vehicles (sizes and volumes) it produces. With fleetwide averaging, a manufacturer can produce some models that exceed their target, and some that are below their target. This approach also helps preserve consumer choice, as the standards do not constrain consumers' opportunity to purchase the size of vehicle with the performance, utility and safety features that meet their needs. In addition, manufacturers have available many other flexibility provisions, including banking and trading of credits across model years and trading credits across manufacturers.

The footprint curves for the MY2012-2025 GHG standards, illustrating the year-over-year stringency increases, are shown below in Figure I.1 and Figure I.2.[28]

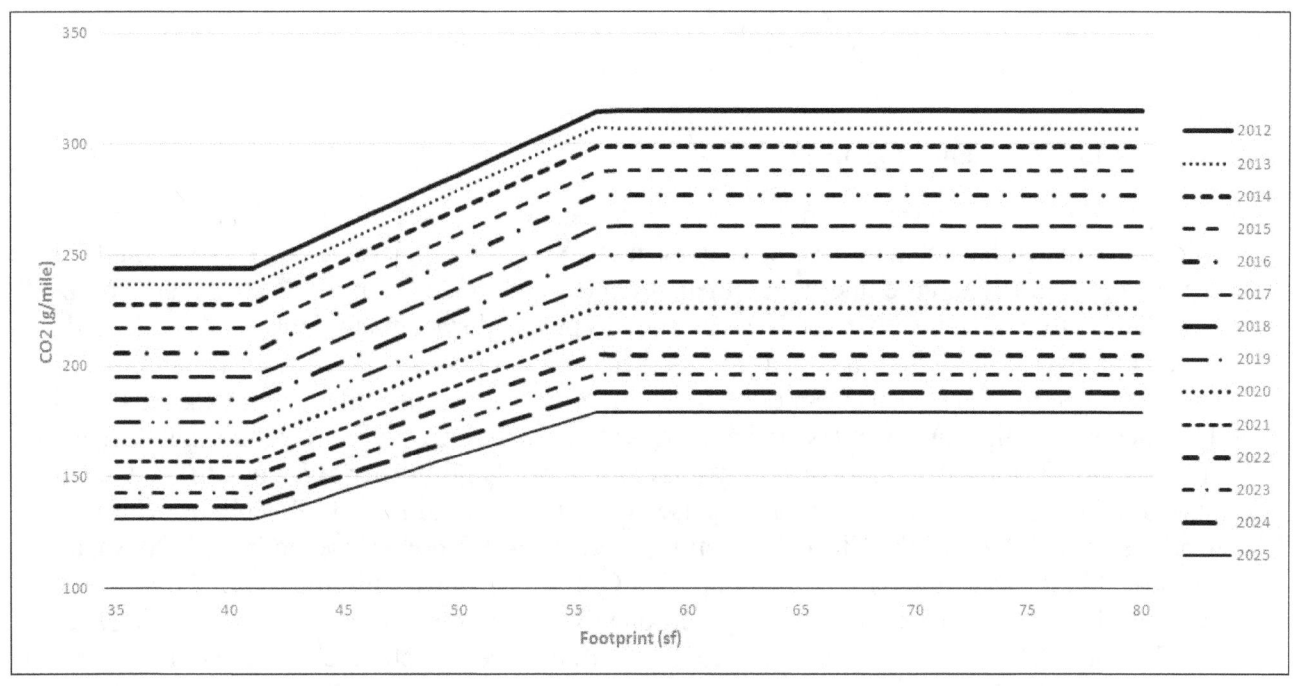

**Figure I.1  CO₂ (g/mile) Passenger Car Standards Curves**

---

[27] Footprint is defined as a vehicle's wheelbase multiplied by its average track width—in other words, the area enclosed by the points at which the wheels meet the ground.
[28] See 40 CFR 86.1818-12(c).

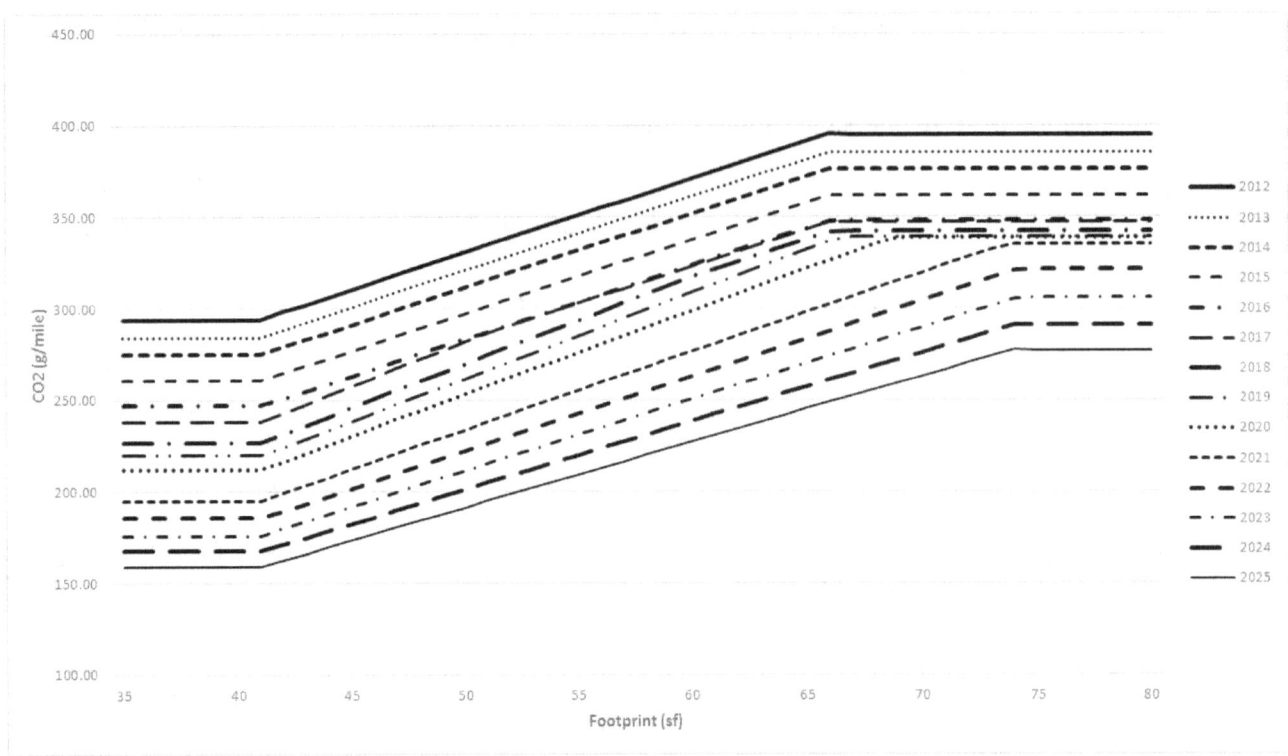

**Figure I.2  CO₂ (g/mile) Light Truck Standards Curves**

## C.    Climate Change Science

In the Proposed Determination, the EPA presented an overview of climate change science as laid out in the climate change assessments from the National Academies, the U.S. Global Change Research Program, and the Intergovernmental Panel on Climate Change.  The EPA summarized the impacts to human health, to ecosystems, and to physical systems in the United States and around the world, from heat waves to sea level rise to disruptions of food security.  Impacts to vulnerable populations such as children, older Americans, persons with disabilities, those with low incomes, indigenous peoples, and persons with preexisting or chronic conditions were also highlighted.  The most recent assessments have confirmed and further expanded the science that supported the 2009 Endangerment and Cause or Contribute Findings for Greenhouse Gases Under section 202(a) of the Clean Air Act; Final Rule (74 FR 66496, December 15, 2009), as discussed in the more recent 2016 Finding That Greenhouse Gas Emissions from Aircraft Cause or Contribute to Air Pollution That May Reasonably Be Anticipated to Endanger Public Health and Welfare (81 FR 54422, August 15, 2016).  Furthermore, the climate system continues to change: in 2015, $CO_2$ concentrations grew by more than 2 parts per million, reaching an annual average of 401 ppm, sea level continued to rise at 3.3 mm/year since the satellite record started in 1993, Arctic sea ice continues to decline, and glaciers continue to melt.[29]  2016 was the

---

[29] Blunden, J. and D. S. Arndt, Eds., 2016: State of the Climate in 2015. Bull. Amer. Meteor. Soc., 97 (8), S1–S275, DOI:10.1175/2016BAMSStateoftheClimate.

warmest year in the global average surface temperature record going back to 1880, the third year in a row of record temperatures.

## II. The Administrator's Assessment of Factors Relevant to the Appropriateness of the MY2022-2025 Standards

Through the Midterm Evaluation, the Administrator must determine whether the GHG standards for model years 2022-2025, established in 2012, are still appropriate, within the meaning of section 202(a)(1) of the Clean Air Act, given the latest available data and information in the record before the Administrator. [30] In this final order, the Administrator is making a final determination that the GHG standards currently in place for MYs 2022-2025 remain appropriate under the Clean Air Act. The consequence of this determination is that the standards remain unchanged, there is no alteration in the rules, and the regulatory status quo continues. The Administrator has fully considered public comments submitted on the Proposed Determination, and the EPA has responded to comments in the accompanying Response to Comments (RTC) document. The Administrator believes that there has been no information presented in the public comments on the Proposed Determination that materially changes the Agency's analysis documented in the Proposed Determination. [31] Therefore, the Administrator considers the analyses presented in the Proposed Determination as the final the EPA analyses upon which this Final Determination is based.

The EPA regulations [32] state that in making the required determination, the Administrator shall consider the information available on the factors relevant to setting greenhouse gas emission standards under section 202(a) of the Clean Air Act for model years 2022 through 2025, including but not limited to:

(i) The availability and effectiveness of technology, and the appropriate lead time for introduction of technology;
(ii) The cost on the producers or purchasers of new motor vehicles or new motor vehicle engines;
(iii) The feasibility and practicability of the standards;
(iv) The impact of the standards on reduction of emissions, oil conservation, energy security, and fuel savings by consumers;
(v) The impact of the standards on the automobile industry;
(vi) The impacts of the standards on automobile safety;
(vii) The impact of the greenhouse gas emission standards on the Corporate Average Fuel Economy standards and a national harmonized program; and
(viii) The impact of the standards on other relevant factors. [33]

---

[30] See 40 CFR 86.1818-12(h).

[31] Proposed Determination on the Appropriateness of the Model Year 2022-2025 Light-Duty Vehicle Greenhouse Gas Emissions Standards under the Midterm Evaluation, EPA-420-R-16-020, and accompanying Technical Support Document, EPA-420-R-16-021, November 2016. In adopting the midterm evaluation provisions, EPA indicated that it "expect[ed] to place primary reliance on peer-reviewed studies" and on "NAS reports" in making midterm evaluation determinations. 77 FR 62787. EPA has in fact done so. See Draft TAR Section 2.2.1 and 2.2.3.

[32] See 40 CFR 86.1818-12(h)(1)(i) through (viii).

[33] 40 CFR 86.1818-12(h)(1).

Below we discuss each of these factors in light of the analyses upon which this Final Determination is based.

*(i) The availability and effectiveness of technology, and the appropriate lead time for introduction of technology; (ii) the cost on the producers or purchasers of new motor vehicles or new motor vehicle engines; (iii) the feasibility and practicability of the standards*

Several of the factors relate to the technology assessment -- technology availability and effectiveness, lead time for introducing technologies, and the costs, feasibility and practicability of the standards. On the basis of EPA's extensive technical analyses contained in the Proposed Determination, and after consideration of the additional comments received by the agency, the Administrator finds that there will be multiple technologies available at reasonable cost to allow the industry to meet the MY2022-2025 standards, with the majority in commercial production today, and others under active development with reliable evidence of feasibility and availability in the market by 2025. See Proposed Determination Sections II and IV.A, and TSD Chapter 2. As in the 2012 FRM, The Administrator further finds that the MY2025 standards can be achieved with very low levels of strong hybrid or plug-in electrified vehicles. The EPA's extensive review of the literature, including but not limited to the 2015 NAS study, makes it clear that advanced gasoline vehicle technologies will continue to improve between now and 2025. In addition, the significant technology advances that have already occurred in just the four years since the 2012 final rule are a strong indication that technology will continue to advance, with clear potential for additional innovation over the next eight years.

The EPA projects a range of potential compliance pathways for each manufacturer and the industry as a whole to meet the MY2022-2025 standards (see Proposed Determination Table IV.5 and Appendix C which show a "central case" and eight sensitivity cases). This analysis indicates that the standards can be met largely through utilization of a suite of advanced gasoline vehicle technologies, with modest penetration of stop-start and mild hybrids and relatively low penetrations of strong hybrids, PHEVs and EVs. The 2015 National Academy of Sciences study on fuel economy technologies similarly found that the 2025 standards would be achieved largely through improvements to a range of technologies that can be applied to a gasoline vehicle without the use of strong hybrids, PHEV, or EV technology. It is important to underscore that EPA's projected technology penetrations are meant to illustrate one of many possible technology pathways to achieve compliance with the MY2022-2025 GHG standards. The rules do not mandate the use of any particular form of technology; the standards are performance-based and thus manufacturers are free to select among the suite of technologies they best believe is right for their vehicles to achieve compliance. As we have seen in recent years with the rapid advances in a wide range of GHG-reduction technologies, we expect that ongoing innovation will result in further improvements to existing technologies and the emergence of others.

As we note throughout this document, the EPA carefully considered and responded in detail to all of the significant public comments as part of the record for the Proposed Determination. Some industry commenters have expressed the view that the EPA did not in fact consider their technical comments. As described in the Proposed Determination and Chapter 2 of the TSD, a number of changes the EPA made to its analysis between the Draft TAR and the Proposed Determination were in response to those technical comments highlighted by the Alliance of Automobile Manufacturers and Global Automakers. These included updating the baseline fleet to a MY2015 basis, better accounting for certain technologies in that baseline fleet, improving the vehicle classification structure to improve the resolution of cost-effectiveness estimates applied in the OMEGA model, updating effectiveness estimates for certain advanced transmission technologies, conducting additional sensitivity analyses (including those where certain advanced technologies are artificially constrained), and adding quality assurance checks of technology effectiveness into the ALPHA and Lumped Parameter Model. See Proposed Determination Appendix A at A-1 and A-2. EPA consulted with NHTSA and CARB as part of the process of developing the Proposed Determination. The Final Determination is based on an administrative record at the very least as robust as that for the 2012 FRM, including extensive state-of-the-art research projects conducted by EPA and consultants to both agencies, data and input from stakeholders, multiple rounds of public comment, information from technical conferences, published literature, and studies published by various organizations. EPA put primary emphasis on the many peer-reviewed studies, as well as on the National Academy of Sciences 2015 report on fuel economy technologies.

Auto industry commenters believe that EPA's analysis generally overestimates the effect of advanced gasoline technologies, that these technologies will not be sufficient to meet the standards, and that higher levels of electrified vehicles will be needed to meet the MY2022-2025 standards. The EPA has carefully considered these comments and our assessment is that the commenters are not considering the possibility of applying the full range of road load reduction and non-electrified powertrain technologies broadly across high volume models, and in the combinations, that the EPA assessed in the Proposed Determination and Draft TAR. In some cases, the auto industry comments, including the Alliance of Automobile Manufacturers (Alliance), are based on the premise that the only possible technologies available in MY2025 will be represented by technology already contained in the fleet today (more specifically, that contained in the Draft TAR's MY2014 baseline fleet), and that those technologies will not improve in efficiency. The EPA disagrees with this assertion; several recently released engines have already demonstrated efficiencies that exceed those in the MY2014 fleet.[34] These actual engines illustrate that improvement has continued beyond the assumed basis of the comments, and it is highly unlikely that even these recent developments represent the limit of achievable efficiencies in the future. EPA's assessment is consistent with the MY2015 NAS report, in which the committee wrote that in the context of increasingly stringent fuel economy and GHG emissions standards, "gasoline-fueled spark ignition (SI) engine will continue to be the dominant powertrain configuration even through 2030 (pg S-1)."[35] Setting aside the assumption that the best available technologies today will undergo no improvement in future years (a premise the auto industry has disproved time and again), the commenters do not even allow for the recombination of existing technologies, and thus severely and unduly limit potential effectiveness increases obtainable by MY2025. The EPA notes that events have already disproven this assumption; as one specific example, Ford introduced a 10-speed automatic transmission on the MY2017 F150 paired with a turbocharged downsized engine, which represents a technology combination that was not previously available and was therefore not considered (and would be deemed impossible) by the Alliance comments. NGO commenters, on

---

[34] These engines include the 1.5L Honda turbo, Volkswagen's EA888-3B Miller cycle, and Hyundai-Kia's 2.0L Atkinson cycle engine.

[35] The 2015 NAS report also included an example technology pathway which illustrated how the application of conventional, non-electrified technologies would enable the example midsize car to meet its MY2025 footprint target (pp 8-18, 8-19).

the other hand, believe that EPA's analysis is robust and that, if anything, EPA's assessment of technologies is overly conservative as we did not consider additional technologies expected to be in the market in the MY2022-2025 timeframe.

The EPA also has carefully considered comments and issues related to powertrain improvements, including advanced engine technologies and improvements to transmission technologies. See 76 FR 48763 and 77 FR 62784. A key technology the EPA assessed in the Draft TAR and Proposed Determination to be available at reasonable cost is the Atkinson Cycle engine in non-hybrid applications. The Atkinson Cycle architecture has already been demonstrated in production domestically (Mazda, Toyota, Hyundai-Kia), enhanced with cooled exhaust gas recirculation (Mazda), and in Europe further enhanced with cylinder deactivation (Volkswagen). These production examples are consistent with EPA engine modeling and initial hardware testing that shows synergies between the use of cooled exhaust gas recirculation and cylinder deactivation with Atkinson Cycle engines. See TSD Chapter 2.3.4.1.4. In addition, and as explained in TSD Chapter 2.3.4.1.8.3 and further below, the EPA conducted sensitivity analyses constraining penetration of Atkinson-cycle engines and found that there are other cost-effective compliance paths available which rely chiefly on engine technology alternatives, rather than on electrification. We did not receive information in the comments on the Proposed Determination that provided a basis for reaching a different conclusion. Among these alternative technology paths are increased penetration of gasoline direct injected, turbo-downsized engines (a chief technology in the agencies' 2012 FRM assessment). The EPA has carefully considered and addressed the comments questioning the effectiveness values the EPA estimated for this technology; the EPA continues to believe these estimates are well grounded. The EPA explained in detail why the engine configuration used in its effectiveness estimates is representative, why the friction reduction assumptions are sound based on the use of coatings and other materials and technologies throughout the engine's moving components, and why the production engines cited as alternatives in the comments are not representative of feasible effectiveness values in 2025 given that they lack various technologies that improve efficiency (including variable valve lift, external cooled exhaust gas recirculation, sequential turbocharging, and higher peak cylinder pressure capability). See TSD Chapter 2.3.4.1.9.1.

The EPA is projecting average per vehicle costs of $875 across the fleet (see Table ES-1 and Proposed Determination Table IV.5).[36] These costs are lower than those projected in the 2012 rule, which the EPA estimated at about $1,100 (see Table 12.44 of the Draft TAR). The EPA found in the 2012 rule that these (higher) costs were reasonable, even without considering the payback in the form of less fuel used, which more than offsets these costs. See 77 FR 62663-62665, 62880 and 62922. Consequently, the EPA regards these lower estimated per-vehicle costs to be reasonable. Furthermore, the projected reduced fuel expenditures more than offset the estimated increase in vehicle cost even with lower assumptions of fuel cost. EPA's analysis finds that consumers who finance their vehicle with a 5-year loan would see payback within the first year; consumers who pay cash for their vehicle would see payback in the fifth year of

---

[36] Across eight sensitivity cases, average per-vehicle costs ranged from $800-$1,115. See Proposed Determination Table IV.5.

ownership. Consumers would realize net savings of $1,650 over the lifetime of their new vehicle (i.e., net of increased lifetime costs and lifetime fuel savings).

This decrease in estimated per-vehicle cost is not surprising—technology to achieve environmental improvements has often proved to be less costly than EPA's initial estimates.[37] Captured in these cost estimates, we project significant increases in the use of advanced engine technologies, comprising more than 60 percent of the fleet across a range of engines including turbo-downsized 18 bar and 24 bar, naturally-aspirated Atkinson cycle, and Miller cycle engines. We also see significant increases of advanced transmission technology projected to be implemented on more than 90 percent of the fleet, which includes continuously variable transmissions (CVTs) and eight-speed automatic transmissions. Stop-start technology and mild hybrid electrification are projected to be used on 15 percent and 18 percent, respectively, of the fleet. Similar to the analysis in the 2012 FRM, the EPA is projecting very low levels of strong hybrids (2 percent) and EV/PHEVs (5 percent) as absolute levels in the fleet (in the central case analysis, see Table ES-1).[38]

The EPA has considered the feasibility of the standards under several different scenarios of future fuel prices and fleet mix, as well as other sensitivity cases (e.g., different assumptions about technologies or credit trading) (see Proposed Determination Section IV.A and Appendix C), which showed only very small variations in average per-vehicle cost or technology penetration mix. Thus, our conclusion that there are multiple ways the MY2022-2025 standards can be met with a wide range of technologies at reasonable cost, and predominantly with advanced engine technologies, holds across all these scenarios.

These technology pathway findings are similar to the types of technologies that EPA projected in establishing the standards in the 2012 rule, although the specific technologies within the advanced engine, advanced transmission, and mild hybrid categories have been updated from the 2012 rule to reflect the current state of technological development (hence the lower estimated per vehicle cost than in the 2012 rule). For example, additional engine technologies, such as the naturally aspirated Atkinson cycle and Miller cycle noted above, were not even considered by the agencies in the 2012 rule yet are in production vehicles today. Similarly, transmission technology has developed such that CVTs are now emerging as a more popular choice for manufacturers than the dual-clutch transmissions we had mainly considered in 2012.[39] Mild hybrid technology also has developed, with more sophisticated 48-volt systems now offering a more cost-effective option than the 110-volt systems we had considered in the 2012 rule. The fact that these technologies have developed and improved so rapidly in the past four years since the MY2022-2025 standards were established provides a strong indication that the pace of innovation is likely to continue. The EPA expects that this trend will continue, likely affording

---

[37] U.S. EPA, National Center for Environmental Economics (2014). "Retrospective Study of the Costs of EPA Regulations: A Report of Four Case Studies." EPA 240-F-14-001, https://yosemite.epa.gov/ee/epa/eerm nsf/vwAN/EE-0575.pdf/$file/EE-0575.pdf including its literature review, Chapter 1.1.

[38] Note that a portion of the five percent EV/PHEV penetration is attributed to the California Zero Emission Vehicle (ZEV) program which is included in our reference case. See TSD Section 1.2.1.1. The incremental penetration of EV/PHEVs needed to meet the EPA GHG standards is projected to be less than one percent. See Proposed Determination Appendix C.1.1.3.2, Tables C.19-C.22, p. A-136-137.

[39] 77 FR 62852-62883; October 15, 2012.

manufacturers even more technology options, and at potentially lower cost, than the Administrator was able to consider at this time for the Final Determination.

EPA's analysis indicates that the effectiveness of the technologies evaluated provides manufacturers with a feasible, reasonable mix of technologies that are predominantly in production today, though not always in combination. For example, a manufacturer may have moved to an advanced turbo-downsized engine design and applied aerodynamic improvements, but not yet applied more advanced transmission or applied further mass reduction opportunities. In addition, there are some straightforward improvements to these technologies that are anticipated and well-documented in the record. See, e.g., Proposed Determination TSD Chapters 2.2.3.4 through 2.2.3.11, and 2.2.7.2 through 2.2.7.5. Most of the automaker comments to the Proposed Determination regarding feasibility did not account for the possibility of using a broad slate of technologies in combination. A few manufacturers have shared with the EPA confidential business information illustrating technology walks (or "techwalks"), which show the cumulative effects of the application of various technologies applied to a given vehicle model. However, while the techwalks provided include some of the same advanced technologies considered by EPA, none of the techwalks include a fuller range of conventional technologies in the combinations described in the Proposed (and Final) Determination. Some are missing very reasonable vehicle technologies, some are missing very reasonable engine technologies, and some are missing very reasonable transmission technologies. Because the manufacturer example techwalks don't include all technologies in the appropriate combinations and in some cases don't include the appropriate credit values, the examples show a shortfall (as would be expected) of about 20-40 g/mi depending on the vehicle. This resulting gap between the EPA and manufacturer-supplied projections would be eliminated if a broader set of the available technologies described in the Final Determination were included in their analysis and appropriate credit values were used.

Moreover, the EPA believes there is ample lead time between now and MY2022-2025 for manufacturers to continue implementing additional technologies into their vehicle production such that the MY2022-2025 standards can be achieved.

In considering whether lead time for the MY2022-2025 standards is adequate, the EPA recognizes that these standards were first established in 2012, providing the auto manufacturers with up to 13 years of lead time for product planning to meet these standards. In the 2012 rule, the EPA concluded that, "EPA agrees that the long lead time in this rulemaking should provide additional certainty to manufacturers in their product planning. The EPA believes that there are several factors that have quickened the pace with which new technologies are being brought to market, and this will also facilitate regulatory compliance."[40] As noted, in setting the standards in 2012, the EPA was beginning to see that technologies were being brought to market at a quickened pace, and this trend has clearly continued over the past four years (see Proposed Determination Section II). The EPA's 2016 $CO_2$ and Fuel Economy Trends report provides even further evidence of the rapid pace at which manufacturers are bringing advanced technologies into the fleet. For example, GM, Honda and Hyundai have implemented advanced transmissions on 80-90 percent of their fleets within the past five years. Over that same period, GM and Ford have implemented turbocharged engines on 25 percent and 40 percent of their fleets,

---

[40] 77 FR 62880; October 15, 2012.

respectively. Given that the EPA projects that the fleet as a whole could reach the 2025 standards with penetrations of 27 percent turbo-downsized 18 bar engines, and 7 percent turbo-downsized 24 bar engines, these penetration rates are clearly achievable given the pace with which some manufacturers have already implemented similar technologies.[41] With respect to the issue of lead time for the Atkinson engine technology, many of the building blocks necessary to operate an engine in Atkinson mode are already present in the MY2016 fleet (including gasoline direct injection (GDI), increased valve phasing authority, higher compression ratios, and (in some instances) cooled exhaust gas recirculation (cEGR)). Some of the potential packaging obstacles mentioned in comments, such as exhaust manifold design, should not be an impediment because more conventional manifold designs (not requiring a revamping of vehicle architecture) are both available and demonstrated in non-hybrid Atkinson cycle applications. There thus should be sufficient lead time before MY2022 to adopt the technology, since it could be incorporated without needing to be part of a major vehicle redesign.

Indeed, technology adoption rates and the pace of innovation have accelerated even beyond what EPA expected when initially setting these standards, which will further aid in addressing any potential for lead time concerns. By the time manufacturers must meet the MY2025 standards, since the standards were set in 2012, they will have had up to 13 years of lead time for product planning and at least 2-3 product redesign cycles, and at present manufacturers still have 5 to 8 years of lead time until the MY2022-2025 standards, with at least 1-2 redesign cycles.[42]

The EPA has also evaluated the progress of the existing fleet in meeting standards in future model years. See the Proposed Determination TSD Appendix C. This assessment shows that more than 100 individual MY2016 vehicle versions, or about 17 percent of the fleet, already meet future footprint-based $CO_2$ targets for MY2020 with current powertrains and air conditioning improvements. These figures do not include off-cycle credits in assessing compliance. In light of the fact that manufacturers are reporting an average of 3 g/mi of off-cycle credits across the fleet for 2015, with some manufacturers reporting more than 4 g/mi off-cycle credits, the share of the MY2016 fleet that can already meet the MY2020 footprint-based $CO_2$ targets -- four years ahead of schedule-- is actually even higher.

Notably, the majority of these vehicles are gasoline powertrains, and the vehicles include nearly every vehicle type, including midsize cars, SUVs, and pickup trucks, and span nearly every major manufacturer. It is important to note that because of the fleetwide averaging structure of the standards, not all vehicles are required to be below their individual targets, and in fact EPA expects that manufacturers will be able to comply with the standards with roughly 50 percent of their production meeting or falling below the footprint based targets. This analysis is another indication that the fleet is on track to meet future standards, especially given the 5 to 8 years of lead time remaining to MY2022-2025.

Consequently, evaluating the factors the EPA is required to consider under 40 CFR 86.1818(h)(1) (i), (ii), and (iii) of the mid-term evaluation rules, based on the current record before the Administrator, there is available and effective technology to meet the MY2022-2025 standards, it is available at reasonable cost to the producers and purchasers of new motor

---

[41] EPA 2016 $CO_2$ and Fuel Economy Trends Report, Figures 6.2, 6.3 and 6.5.

[42] Redesign cycles are summarized in the Proposed Determination Appendix A and are discussed in greater detail in the 2012 FRM final Joint Technical Support Document, EPA-420-R-12-901, at Chapter 3.5.1.

vehicles or new motor vehicle engines, there is adequate lead time to meet those standards, and the standards are thus feasible and practicable. Moreover, this most recent analysis remains consistent with the key conclusions reached in the 2012 FRM: there are multiple compliance paths based chiefly on deployment of advanced gasoline engine technologies with minimal needed penetration of strong hybrid or full electric vehicles, projected per vehicle costs are lower than in the 2012 FRM, and the cost of the lower emitting technology is fully paid back by the associated fuel savings.

*(iv) The impact of the standards on reduction of emissions, oil conservation, energy security, and fuel savings by consumers*

The EPA also has considered the impact of the standards on reduction of emissions, oil conservation, energy security, and fuel savings by consumers, again as required by the Midterm Evaluation rules. Light-duty vehicles are significant contributors to the U.S. GHG emissions inventory—responsible for 61 percent of U.S. transportation GHG emissions and 16 percent of total U.S. GHG emissions in 2014—and thus must be a critical part of any program to reduce U.S. GHG emissions. EPA projects that the MY2022-2025 standards will reduce GHG emissions annually by more than 230 million metric tons (MMT) by 2050, and nearly 540 MMT over the lifetime of MY2022-2025 vehicles. See Proposed Determination Section IV.A.4, Table IV.6, and Appendix C.2. These projected GHG reductions associated with the MY2022-2025 standards are significant compared to total light-duty vehicle GHG emissions of 1,100 MMT in 2014.[43] See Proposed Determination Section IV and Table IV.6.

These standards are projected to reduce oil consumption by 50 billion gallons and to save U.S. consumers nearly $92 billion in fuel cost over the lifetime of MY2022-2025 vehicles. See Proposed Determination Table IV.8 and IV.13, respectively. On average for a MY2025 vehicle (compared to a vehicle meeting the MY2021 standards), consumers will save more than $2,800 in total fuel costs over that vehicle's lifetime, with a net savings of $1,650 after taking into consideration the upfront increased vehicle costs. See Proposed Determination Table IV.12, 3 percent discount rate case. EPA considers a range of societal benefits of the standards, including the social costs of carbon and other GHGs, health benefits, energy security, the value of time saved for refueling, and others.

Benefits are projected to far outweigh the costs, with net benefits totaling nearly $100 billion over the lifetime of MY2022-2025 vehicles (3 percent discount rate). See Proposed Determination Section IV.A.6 and Table IV.13. As was the case when the EPA first established the MY2022-2025 standards in the 2012 rule, this analysis also supports a conclusion that the standards remain appropriate – and indeed will provide enormous benefits -- from the standpoint of impacts of the standards on emissions, oil conservation, energy security, and fuel savings.

*(v) The impact of the standards on the automobile industry*

EPA has assessed the impacts of the standards on the automobile industry. We have estimated the costs required to meet the MY2022-2025 standards at about $33 billion (see

---

[43] Inventory of U.S. Greenhouse Gas Emissions and Sinks: 1990-2014, EPA 430-R-16-002, April 15, 2016.

Proposed Determination Section IV.A and Table IV.13), with an average per-vehicle cost of about $875 (see Proposed Determination Section IV.A and Tables IV.4 and IV.5). These costs are less than those originally projected when the EPA first established these standards in the 2012 rule; at that time, we had projected an average per vehicle cost of approximately $1,100 (see Table 12.44 of the Draft TAR). The Administrator found those (higher) projected costs to be reasonable in the 2012 rule, and finds the lower projected costs shown in our current analysis continues to support the appropriateness of the standards.

In addition to costs, the EPA has assessed impacts on the auto industry in terms of potential impacts on vehicle sales. See Proposed Determination Section III and Appendix B and TSD Chapter 4. As part of these assessments, the EPA has evaluated a range of issues affecting consumers′ purchases of vehicles, which also addresses a portion of the factor, "the cost on the producers or purchasers of new motor vehicles or new motor vehicle engines" (emphasis added, 40 CFR 86.1818-12(h)(ii)). EPA's assessments indicate that, to date, there is little, if any, evidence that consumers have experienced adverse effects from the standards. Vehicle sales continue to be strong, with annual increases for seven straight years, through 2016, for the first time in 100 years, and record sales in 2016. These sales increases are likely due not to the standards, but rather to economic recovery from the 2008-2009 recession. Nevertheless, at the least, we find no evidence that the standards have impeded sales. We also have not found any evidence that the technologies used to meet the standards have imposed "hidden costs" in the form of adverse effects on other vehicle attributes. See Proposed Determination Appendix B.1.4 and B.1.5.2. Similarly, we have not identified significant effects on vehicle affordability to date. See Proposed Determination Appendix B.1.6. We recognize that the standards will have some impact on the price of new vehicles, but we do not believe that the standards have significantly reduced the availability of vehicle model choices for consumers at any particular price point, including the lowest price vehicle segment. Id. at Appendix B.1.6.1. Given the lead time provided since the 2012 rule for automakers to achieve the MY2022-25 standards, and the evidence to date of consumer acceptance of technologies being used to meet the standards, the EPA expects that any effects of the standards on the vehicle market will be small relative to market responses to broader macroeconomic conditions.

The main argument in the public comments on both the Draft TAR and the Proposed Determination that the standards will have an adverse impact on the industry is that the standards, although achievable, will require extensive electrification of the fleet to do so, and this will result in more expensive vehicles -- and an emerging technology -- which consumers will be reluctant to purchase. Our analysis, however, indicates that there are multiple compliance pathways which would need only minimal (less than 3 percent) of strong hybrids and electric vehicles, and that the great bulk of technologies used would be based on improvements to gasoline internal combustion engines. This is true not only in the agency's primary analysis, but also in a series of sensitivity analyses (assuming, among other things, significantly less use of the Atkinson engine technology, and a wide range of fuel prices). See Table ES-1 and the Proposed Determination Section IV.A.3 and Appendix C.1. This analysis is also consistent with findings of the 2015 NAS study (as well as each agency's findings in the 2012 FRM).[44] Consequently, the EPA does believe that the evidence supports the claim of the comments on this point.

---

[44] "Cost, Effectiveness and Deployment of Fuel Economy Technologies for Light-Duty Vehicles," National Research Council of the National Academies, June 2015.

The EPA also carefully considered the issue of whether there has been consumer acceptance of the new fuel efficiency technologies. As noted, industry sales are at a record high, with sales increasing for seven consecutive years for the first time since the 1920's. These sales trends provide no evidence of consumer reluctance to purchase the new technologies. Moreover, professional auto reviews found generally positive associations with the existence of the technologies. See Section B.1.5.1.2 of the Appendix to the Proposed Determination. The evidence to date thus supports consumer acceptance of the new technologies.

Another potential impact on the automobile industry that the EPA has assessed is the potential for impacts on employment. EPA's assessment projects job growth in the automotive manufacturing sector and automotive parts manufacturing sector due specifically to the need to increase expenditures for the vehicle technologies needed to meet the standards. We do not attempt to quantitatively estimate the total effects of the standards on the automobile industry, due to the significant uncertainties underlying any estimate of the impacts of the standards on vehicle sales. Nor do we quantitatively estimate the total effects on employment at the national level, because such effects depend heavily on the state of overall employment in the economy. We further note that, under conditions of full employment, any changes in employment levels in the regulated sector due to the standards are mostly expected to be offset by changes in employment in other sectors. See the Proposed Determination Appendix B.2. The Administrator finds that, while the standards are likely to have some effect on employment, this effect (whether positive or negative) is likely to be small enough that it will be unable to be distinguished from other factors affecting employment, especially macroeconomic conditions and their effect on vehicle sales.

The Administrator thus finds, based on the current record, that the standards will impose reasonable per vehicle costs (and less than those projected in the 2012 FRM), that there is no evidence of the standards having an adverse impact on vehicle sales or on other vehicle attributes, or on employment in the automotive industry sector. Given these assessments of potential impacts on costs to the auto industry and average per-vehicle costs, consumers' purchases of vehicles, and employment, the Administrator finds that the potential impacts on the automobile industry support a conclusion that the MY2022-2205 standards remain appropriate and should not be changed.

*(vi) The impacts of the standards on automobile safety*

The EPA has assessed the potential impacts of the standards on automobile safety. In the Proposed Determination, consistent with the Draft TAR's safety assessment, the EPA assessed the potential of the MY2022-2025 standards to affect vehicle safety. In the Draft TAR (Chapter 8), the agencies reviewed the relationships between mass, size, and fatality risk based on the statistical analysis of historical crash data, which included a new analysis performed by using the most recent available crash data. The EPA used this updated analysis[45] in the Proposed Determination to calculate the estimated safety impacts of the modeled mass reductions over the lifetimes of new vehicles in response to MY2022-2025 standards. See the Proposed

---

[45] Puckett, S.M. and Kindelberger, J.C. (2016, June). Relationships between Fatality Risk, Mass, and Footprint in Model Year 2003-2010 Passenger Cars and LTVs – Preliminary Report. Washington, DC: National Highway Traffic Safety Administration.

Determination Section III.C.1 and Appendix B.3.1. EPA's analysis finds that the fleet can achieve modest levels of mass reduction as one technology among many to meet the MY2022-2025 standards without any net increase in fatalities. The 2015 NAS study further found that the footprint-based standards are likely to have little effect on vehicle and overall highway safety.[46] Therefore, the Administrator finds that the existing MY2022-2025 standards will have no adverse impact on automobile safety. There is no evidence in the public comments that suggests a different conclusion.

*(vii) The impact of the greenhouse gas emission standards on the corporate average fuel economy standards and a national harmonized program*

The EPA has assessed the impacts of the standards on the CAFE standards and a national harmonized program. EPA notes that NHTSA has established augural standards for MY2022-2025 and must by statute undertake a *de novo* notice and comment rulemaking to establish final standards for these model years. Under the Energy Policy and Conservation Act (EPCA) statute, as amended by the Energy Independence and Security Act (EISA), NHTSA must establish final standards at least 18 months before the beginning of each model year.[47] That statute requires the Secretary of Transportation to consult with the EPA Administrator in establishing fuel economy standards.[48] The EPCA/EISA statute includes a number of factors that NHTSA must consider in deciding maximum feasible average fuel economy, including "the effect of other motor vehicle standards of the Government on fuel economy."[49] Thus, in determining the CAFE standards for MY2022-2025, NHTSA can take into consideration the light-duty GHG standards, and indeed did so in initially establishing the MY2017-2021 CAFE standards and the augural MY2022-2025 standards. See 77 FR 62669, 62720, 62803-804. The EPA believes that by providing information on our evaluation of the current record and our determination that the existing GHG standards for MY2022-2025 are appropriate, we are enabling, to the greatest degree possible, NHTSA to take this analysis and the GHG standards into account in considering the appropriate CAFE standards for MY2022-2025.

The EPA recognizes that in 2012, when we discussed the mid-term evaluation, we expressed an intent that if EPA's determination was that the standards should not change, the EPA would issue its final determination concurrently with NHTSA's final rule adopting fuel economy standards for MY2022-2025. See 77 FR at 62633. Our intent was to align the agencies' proceedings for MYs 2022-2025 and to maintain a joint national program. *Id.* The EPA remains committed to a joint national program that aligns, as much as possible, the requirements of EPA, NHTSA, and CARB. The Administrator concludes, however, that providing her determination that the GHG standards remain appropriate now, rather than waiting until after NHTSA has proposed standards, allows NHTSA to fully account for the GHG standards and is more likely to align the agencies' determinations. Thus, the Administrator finds that her determination takes

---

[46] "Cost, Effectiveness and Deployment of Fuel Economy Technologies for Light-Duty Vehicles," National Research Council of the National Academies, June 2015, Finding 10.2.

[47] 42 U.S.C. 32902(a).

[48] 42 U.S.C. 32902(b)(1).

[49] 42 U.S.C. 32902(f).

account of the relationship between GHG standards and fuel economy standards and supports the goal of a national harmonized program.[50]

In an action separate from this Final Determination, the EPA will be responding to a petition received from the auto industry trade associations, the Alliance of Automobile Manufacturers and Global Automakers, regarding several provisions that they request be harmonized between the EPA GHG standards and the NHTSA CAFE standards.[51] On December 21, 2016, NHTSA signed a Federal Register notice signaling its plan to consider the NHTSA-specific requests from the auto industry petition. The EPA likewise intends, in the near future, to continue working together with NHTSA, the Petitioners and other stakeholders, as we carefully consider the requests made in the June 2016 petition, and possible ways to further harmonize the national program.

### (viii) The impact of the standards on other relevant factors

In addition to the above factors, the Administrator has also considered the factor of regulatory certainty -- which relates closely to the issue of lead time discussed above. Regulatory certainty gives the automakers the time they need to conduct long-term planning and engineering to meet future standards. Indeed, the 2012 standards covered a long period of time – 13 years—in order to provide the industry with a lengthy period of stability and certainty. Thus, the Midterm Evaluation called for rule changes only if the Administrator found the existing standards to be no longer feasible and appropriate. Clearly, as discussed above, the automakers' response to technology development and deployment in the face of the regulatory certainty provided by the MY2012-2021 standards, which are not subject to the midterm evaluation, has exceeded EPA's projections set out in the original 2012 rule. Having the same certainty on the level of the MY2022-2025 standards can now enable manufacturers to continue unimpeded their existing long-term product planning and technology development efforts, which, in turn, could lead to even further, and perhaps sooner, breakthroughs in technology. These efforts could contribute to the continued success of the industry and the GHG standards program, which in turn would benefit consumers through fuel savings and the public through reduced emissions. Initiating a rulemaking now to change the standards would disrupt the industry's planning for future product lines and investments. Thus, the Administrator finds that regulatory certainty is an important consideration in assessing the appropriateness of the standards.

---

[50] The MTE rules themselves do not require concurrent timing with any aspect of NHTSA's rulemaking. Moreover, there is uncertainty as to whether the NHTSA rulemaking would be complete by the date on which EPA is mandated to make a final determination, so that the expressed hope (in the 2012 preamble) of concurrent proceedings may be overtaken by events in any case.

[51] "Petition for Direct Final Rule with Regard to Various Aspects of the Corporate Average Fuel Economy Program and the Greenhouse Gas Program," submitted by the Alliance of Automobile Manufacturers and the Association of Global Automakers to EPA and NHTSA, June 20, 2016.

## III. Final Determination

Having considered available information on each of the above factors required by the regulations, under 40 CFR 86.1818-12(h)(1), the Administrator is determining that the GHG standards currently in place for MYs 2022-2025 are appropriate under section 202(a)(1) and (2) of the Clean Air Act. The Administrator has fully considered public comments submitted on the Proposed Determination, and there has been no information provided through the comments that compels or persuades the Administrator to alter her Proposed Determination. The consequence of this final determination is a continuation of the current regulatory status quo. The regulations themselves are unaltered as a result of this determination.

In the Administrator's view, the record clearly establishes that, in light of technologies available today and improvements we project will occur between now and MY2022-2025, it will be practical and feasible for automakers to meet the MY2022-2025 standards at reasonable cost that will achieve the significant GHG emissions reduction goals of the program, while delivering significant reductions in oil consumption and associated fuel savings for consumers, significant benefits to public health and welfare, and without having material adverse impact on the industry, safety, or consumers. The Administrator recognizes that not all of the technologies available today have been implemented in a widespread manner, but she also recognizes that the purpose of the Midterm Evaluation is to assess whether the standards remain appropriate in light of the pace of compliance and technological development in the industry. As discussed above, the technological development of advanced gasoline vehicle technologies has surpassed EPA's expectations when we initially adopted the standards. Although we anticipated in 2012 that the standards could be met primarily using advanced gasoline engine and transmission technologies, the range of technology development has been more extensive and effective than anticipated. The industry's vibrancy, initiative, and ingenuity is to be commended. The Administrator concludes that the MY2022-2025 standards could be largely met simply by implementation of these technologies, but we recognize that we are at the mid-point of these standards phasing-in and it would be unreasonable, in light of past developments, ongoing investment by the industry, and EPA's extensive review of the literature on future technologies and improvements to existing technologies, to expect that no further technology development would occur that could be implemented for MY2022-2025 vehicles. In the Draft TAR and Proposed Determination, the EPA was not even able to consider all of the technologies being developed because of the rapid pace of development. As discussed in the Proposed Determination (see Section II and Appendix B), the EPA did not consider several technologies that we know are under active development and may potentially provide additional cost-effective technology pathway options for meeting the MY2025 standards; examples of such technologies include electric boosting, dynamic cylinder deactivation, and variable compression ratio. A significant difference between the industry analysis and that of the EPA is over the extent to which electric vehicle production will be needed to meet the standards. Many of industry's comments regarding cost, consumer acceptance, and other factors primarily stem from their view that significant EV penetration will be required. As discussed earlier, the Administrator has considered the report of the National Academy of Sciences and information and data from the auto industry, and she has determined based on the technical record before her that the industry's conclusions do not take into account the possibility of applying the full range of road load reduction and non-electrified powertrain technologies broadly across high volume models, and in the combinations, that the EPA assessed in the Proposed Determination and Draft TAR. In addition, the automotive industry has been characterized throughout its history by continued innovation and adoption of ever-improving technologies to improve fuel economy and lower emissions while simultaneously providing a range of vehicles to customers with the features they desire (safety, driveability, etc.). Thus, in light of the pace of progress in reducing GHG emissions since the MY2022-2025 standards were adopted, the success of automakers in achieving the standards to date while vehicle sales are strong, the projected costs of the standards, the impact of the standards on reducing emissions and fuel costs for consumers, and the other factors identified in 40 CFR 86.1818-12(h) and discussed above, the Administrator concludes that the record does not support a conclusion that the MY2022-2025 standards should be revised to make them less stringent.

The Administrator has also considered whether, in light of these factors and the record (including public comments urging more stringent standards), it would be appropriate to make the standards more stringent. She recognizes that the current record, including the current state of technology and the pace of technology development and implementation, could support a decision to adopt more stringent standards for MY2022-2025 (or, put more precisely, could support a decision to initiate rulemaking proposing to amend the standards to increase their stringency). The EPA found in 2012 that the projected standards were feasible at reasonable cost, and the current record shows that the standards are feasible at even less cost and that there are more available technologies (particularly advanced gasoline technologies) than projected in 2012, and that the benefits outweigh the costs by nearly $100 billion. These factors could be the basis for a proposal to amend the standards to increase the standards' stringency. Moreover, one could point to the overall need to significantly reduce greenhouse gases in the transportation sector even further, especially given expected growth in vehicle travel. The Administrator also recognizes, however, that regulatory certainty is an important and critical consideration. Regulatory certainty gives the automakers the time they need to conduct long-term planning and engineering that could lead to major advancements in technology while contributing to the continued success of the industry and the GHG standards program, which in turn will benefit consumers and reduce emissions. She also believes a decision to maintain the current standards provides support to a timely NHTSA rulemaking to adopt MY2022-2025 standards and a harmonized national program. Thus, the Administrator has concluded that it is appropriate to provide the full measure of lead time for the MY2022-2025 standards, rather than initiating rulemaking to adopt new, more stringent standards with a shorter lead time and significant uncertainty in the interim which would impede on-going technological improvements and innovation.

Accordingly, the Administrator concludes that in light of all the prescribed factors, and considering the entire record, the current MY2022-2025 standards are appropriate.